THE SECRET OF BITCOIN

SATOSHI SEO

nummum
EDITORIAL

CONTENTS

INTRODUCTION TO BITCOIN

In 2008, bitcoin appeared on the world financial market, which stood out as the first independent proposal to create a cryptocurrency that would serve as a payment system and commodity.

The first transaction in bitcoins was made on January 3, 2009 through the Sourceforge portal, a web platform specializing in the creation of open source software.

On that day, the first 50 bitcoins were sold to the public. Today, a total of 128 million bitcoins, whose official denomination is BTC, are managed in the cryptocurrency market.

Most importantly, this amount will neither increase nor decrease (at least for now).

Another interesting thing is that nobody knows exactly who invented it, as the name of the supposed creator, Satoshi Nakamoto, turned out to be a pseudonym.

Bitcoin has several things that make it special, starting with the fact that its value is not determined by any central bank or public or private financial institution.

Instead, its value comes from the trust placed in it by

users who use it as a form of payment for products or services.

It should be noted that bitcoin transactions do not need to be validated by a currency exchange system or a bank. To certify each transaction, it has its own platform based on a complex validation process through peer-to-peer networks called Blockchain Bitcoin.

In this paper we will explain in detail what bitcoin is, why it is so important in today's financial world and how you can use it as an alternative to traditional payment systems.

THE IMPACT OF BITCOIN ON THE WORLD ECONOMY

The emergence of Bitcoin in 2008 opened the door to a new way of exchanging goods and services beyond payment with traditional money, stocks or securities.

Thanks to Bitcoin, cryptocurrencies are accepted and used today in countless activities. Gone are the days when investments and businesses were based only on FIAT money, i.e. money printed and managed by central banks.

In 2021, bitcoin remains by far the most widely used and most important virtual currency in the global financial system.

And its impact is not only limited to individuals or companies that use it as a currency. Even countries with problems of devaluation of their national currencies have opted for bitcoin as an alternative to give stability, at least in part, to their financial system.

But what stands out the most, is that many saw Bitcoin and other cryptocurrencies as a viable and advantageous alternative to protect themselves from future global crises similar to the real estate price crash of 2008, which generated the bankruptcy of thousands of banks and credit institutions around the world.

HOW IS BITCOIN DRIVING GLOBAL FINANCIAL TRANSFORMATION?

If you are wondering how a cryptocurrency that is only a few years old can affect the global economy, the answer is simpler than you think.

In today's global and highly technological economy, three major conditions have been created that all economic players must meet if they do not want to be left out of the competition:

- The use of the Internet and information technologies have made the physical boundaries between buyers and sellers disappear. It is imperative to implement efficient and fast e-commerce, just as face-to-face sales were once a priority.
- The market is no longer local or national, it is now global. This makes it necessary to find new ways to sell products and make them arrive quickly regardless of the distance.
- It is necessary to be more competitive, which implies reducing costs and increasing profit margins. An important factor here is to protect oneself from the fluctuations of formal currencies and bank operating costs.

Bitcoin and cryptoassets enable economic actors to meet these assumptions quickly and efficiently.

CHANGES BROUGHT ABOUT BY BITCOIN IN THE PERSONAL ECONOMY

Until the emergence of cryptocurrencies as a mass-use financial and monetary tool, almost all individuals and entities in the world kept their capital in physical money, securities or bonds.

Although the resource of storing gold, silver and other valuable minerals has also been managed, in many countries this is not legal or there are strong inconveniences when using them for the purchase of goods or payment of services.

The increasingly low trust in banks has led millions of people to store their income in a Bitcoin or other cryptocurrency wallet.

This is because there they will be safe from the effects of inflation, devaluation and above all, far from the reach of governments and official entities that they do not trust.

Moreover, they know that the value of their capital in cryptoassets will depend solely on the supply and demand of the market, which is managed by the users themselves.

CHANGES AT THE COMPANY LEVEL

Every day the number of companies accepting bitcoins as a form of payment for their goods and services increases, alongside FIAT money such as the euro, the US dollar and other national currencies.

In addition to the reasons already stated for this massive acceptance of bitcoin, the fact that transactions can be made from anywhere in the world, with total security and in a very short time, also plays an important role.

But what many consider to be Bitcoin's greatest effect on the global economy is that it has spurred the use of direct payments through peer-to-peer (P2P) technology, taking advantage of the ever-improving and more widespread global computer network.

This has grown bitcoin's presence in the market and

pushed its value in recent years to a level never before imagined.

BITCOIN'S ROLE IN A WORLD AFFECTED BY COVID-19

Bitcoin has an important role to play in an economy affected globally by the Covid-19 pandemic. And there are several reasons for this.

First of all, let us remember that before the pandemic was declared in early 2020, the whole world was facing the arrival of a major devaluation of the US dollar, which would affect trade and the relationship between the world's major currencies.

The reason was that the U.S. Federal Reserve began printing large amounts of FIAT dollars in order to pay for the gigantic expenses of the Federal Government, its enormous military budget and the innumerable subsidies given to private corporations in that country.

This caused an increase in inflation in the United States and a devaluation of the dollar, affecting tens of thousands of small and medium-sized companies in that country and, by extension, harming the economies of countries that depend on exports of raw materials or manufactured products to the United States.

This is compounded by the constant variation in oil prices, which tend to remain low, affecting producing countries, which in turn tend to be the main buyers of goods worldwide.

WILL BITCOIN SAVE THE WORLD DURING THE PANDEMIC?

In these circumstances, many investors are betting on Bitcoin as a lifeline that will get them through the pandemic.

One of the biggest advocates of Bitcoin use at the moment is billionaire venture capitalist and technology investor Tim Drapper, who said that it will not be banks or governments that save the day, but Bitcoin.

In case you don't know who this venture capitalist is, we will tell you that he is a graduate of the prestigious universities of Harvard and Stanford, who amassed his fortune by buying shares in Hotmail, Skype and Tesla Motors.

He currently resides in Silicon Valley, California, the largest technological development center in the United States.

In 2014 he became famous as the sole buyer of an auction of 30,000 bitcoins that the US government had seized from the Silk Road company and which at the time were valued at US$17 million (today about US$1.6 billion).

Drapper is an "evangelist" of cryptocurrencies and had already "predicted" that Bitcoin would reach US$10,000 per unit in 2017, which it did. Now he assures that in 2022 it will reach up to US$250,000, which explains his great confidence in this cryptocurrency.

CRYPTOCURRENCIES ACCELERATED GLOBAL ECONOMIC TRANSFORMATION

Many experts believe that the Covid-19 pandemic only accelerated something that was bound to happen sooner or later, the transformation of the world economy and the end of the great financial monopolies.

While there is no clear estimate of how long it will take for this transformation to materialize, it is clear that after the pandemic trade and investment will not be handled as before and bitcoin will play an increasing role in commercial exchange.

Even the swings in value that Bitcoin and other currencies such as Ethereum and Riple suffered in March 2021 did not affect its strength, which far outstrips several traditional currencies that have seen their value decline in recent times.

And this proves that the creators of Bitcoin were not wrong when they stated in 2008 that this cryptocurrency was designed to transform the financial system and protect humanity's capital from the imbalances of the traditional economy.

3

TIPS AND TRICKS TO OBTAIN BITCOINS

Something you probably don't know is that there is more than one way to get bitcoins, apart from buying them. And the best thing is that in many cases this can be done for free or at a very low cost.

Let's first clarify that getting bitoins at bargain prices or for free is not a quick or easy task, but it can be done with relative ease and a little patience.

When a new cryptocurrency comes on the market, several projects or websites appear willing to give away a certain amount to the public, as a way to promote the use of these new forms of value and digital commerce.

Faucets" or some form of "airdrops" are generally used for this. If you don't remember what these things are, check the glossary in Chapter II.

FAUCETS AND AIRDROPS

Since Bitcoin started trading, many faucets (applications and websites) have appeared offering small amounts of this digital asset. All that was required was to view a complete advertisement or fill in a captcha.

Initially, amounts of between 5 to 10 bitcoins were given away, as it should be remembered that this cryptocurrency was extremely cheap in its beginnings and few were convinced to use it.

Although today it is possible to find applications or websites that still offer free bitcoins, they are limited to only a few satoshis at a time. This is still attractive considering how much a bitcoin is worth today.

However, a key point to keep in mind is that there are many other cryptocurrencies that can also be obtained through faucets and airdrops and then exchanged for bitcoins.

Therefore, take advantage of any website that offers you cryptocurrencies for free and keep the reward in your wallet.

And above all, remember to store them in the official wallet of each one or in a recognized wallet, so that you will not have problems in the future.

WHAT FAUCETS CAN YOU USE TO EARN BITCOINS?

We are going to tell you about some airdrops and faucets that you can use to get some free bitcoins.

Freebitcoin

It is a faucet operating since 2012 that works as a kind of lottery. Every 60 minutes you have the opportunity to play. Depending on the number you draw, you will win a greater or lesser amount of satochis.

The only condition to play is to solve a captcha on screen. An attraction of this faucet is that in each spin you will win ticktes for a weekly draw, as well as points that you can exchange for different prizes when you accumulate enough of them.

It also has a system by which you can invite your friends and acquaintances and earn a commission every time they play.

And another advantage is that it will pay you daily interest if you save your balance in the virtual account that you will open in this application. For this, you must have saved a minimum of 30,000 satoshis (0.0003 BTC).

Cointiply

It is a website created by a community of over 1 million users. Contiply offers different ways to accumulate bitocoins every day and earnings can be withdrawn using a Bitocoin wallet, DOGE or the FaucetHub virtual wallet.

To win your prize, you will need to complete online surveys, install and test applications on your mobile device, watch advertisements, play various games or simply watch videos.

Once this is done, you will be able to cash out your "profit". But if you keep this balance in your Cointiply wallet, you will be paid interest.

BTCClicks

Another web-based faucet gives you the opportunity to earn fractions of satoshis for visiting and staying a minimum time on pages that talk about or relate to the critptovalues.

It is a very simple page where you will earn bitcoins for visiting websites that are related to the world of cryptocurrencies.

You will have to stay several seconds on each website and in return you will be able to charge up to 0.00006 mBTC for each ad you click on.

If you want to earn more you can buy a membership for 14.58 mBTC (about 7 dollars). With this membership you are entitled to earn double for each click for a period of 90 days.

CryptoTap Browser, mine bitcoins from a mobile device

The times when you needed a powerful computer to mine bitcoins are long gone. Now you can do it with your latest generation cell phone or tablet using CryptoTap Browser.

This browser will use the processor power of your device to mine bitcoins while browsing your usual pages or even while idle.

It also has the option to invite your contact list and form a network to mine bitcoins collaboratively!

Univox

Another faucet-like website that allows you to earn US dollars payable by PayPal, which you can easily exchange into bitcoins whenever you wish.

Univox will present you with several ways to earn money. The first is to pay $2 for signing up and completing your profile.

You can also receive the equivalent of $0.50 to $4 for answering different types of surveys and between $1 to $10 for spinning a Russian roulette wheel every 24 hours.

You can even earn $1 for each friend you invite who answers at least one of the surveys published on this page.

AIRDROPS, THE OTHER WAY TO GET BITCOINS

As you saw in Chapter II (Vocabulary of the alt-coin ecosystem), an airdrop is a method used by various projects to distribute tokens for free in a set of virtual wallets.

In general, airdrops are used by companies or organizations that want to publicize new projects and seek to interest the largest number of Internet users. An example could be the launch of a new cryptocurrency.

The airdrop is configured to give away

cryptocurrencies or fractions thereof to users who meet certain basic conditions.

Some of the most commonly used are sharing content on your social networks, visiting a link related to the project that manages the airdrop, answering a questionnaire or even purchasing a product or service and registering this purchase to receive a prize.

You may even only be asked to store part of your cryptocurrencies in the wallet of the company or site that manages the airdrop. When it is certified that you have done this action, it proceeds to deliver the promised tokens.

If you are interested in finding out which airdrops are up and running on the Internet or are on their way, you can visit bitcointalk.org and airdropalert.com, where they are often advertised.

MINING BITCOINS, A SAFE WAY TO INCREASE YOUR CAPITAL

Mining bitcoins is a safe way to increase your assets, but it requires a prior investment in equipment and software, which you should consider thoroughly.

Recall that mining is the process of lending your computing power (your computers) to perform the complex mathematical operations required to validate, certify and seal each block of data on a blockchain.

In return, you will receive a certain amount of tokens for each amount of information processed, which you can store in your virtual wallet.

There are two ways to mine bitcoins, hardware and software. Let's see what they are.

Hardware bitcoin mining

If you are interested in hardware mining, you will need to invest in very powerful computing equipment and a good internet connection. This equipment will be dedicated 24 hours a day in the execution of blockchain validation.

You can buy ready-made equipment for cryptocurrency mining, called ASICs such as the famous DragonMint and AntMiner. These are devices that come ready to be connected in series and start mining bitcoins in a few minutes.

But if you are computer literate enough, you can build a set of computers to your liking, using powerful graphics cards (GPUs) from NVIDIA and AMD.

These cards feature very powerful processors, originally designed for the complex 3D drawing operations of modern video games. Thanks to special software their processors can be used to perform the demanding calculations required in the validation and certification of a blockchain.

Whatever the option, we are talking about equipment that generates a high temperature and requires a well-ventilated or cooled installation. They also consume a large amount of electricity, which will result in a high bill every month.

Bitcoin mining in the cloud

This is an interesting option for those who do not want to invest in expensive computer equipment for bitcoin mining.

This involves contracting the mining with a specialized company that has a large amount of equipment or hardware ready for this task.

In short, you would be contracting the rental of a certain amount of "cloud mining capacity" for a specific period of time.

Cloud mining companies have large facilities full of modern equipment for mining cryptocurrencies, called mining farms.

In any case, it must be taken into account that the profitability is much lower than if you use your own equipment and will be affected by the fluctuations of the cryptocurrency market value or the level of commissions to be paid.

Even encountering chains that are more difficult to mine can affect your earnings, if it consumes a good part of the time you have contracted.

LEND YOUR BITCOINS AND EARN INTEREST

If you already have a certain amount of bitcoins in your personal wallet, you can think about investing them in a loan system aimed at people who need this money for a specific purchase or business.

The advantage of this type of service is that you will see your capital increase with the payment of interest according to the amount of bitcoins you lend and the time you set for their repayment.

Remember that bitcoin is money and as such you can use it as capital for a term loan business with variable interest rates.

Where can I bid my bitcoins to lend them at interest?

There are online services that allow you to bid your bitcoins at an interest rate that you consider convenient for you. However, remember that you will not be the only one to bid your bitcoins on these sites and your interest rate should therefore be more attractive than others.

These services will allow you to set the interest rate you want, the amount you will lend and the time you expect your money to be repaid.

It should be noted that these platforms charge a small commission as "intermediaries", but in exchange they guarantee the security of your cryptocurrencies. Examples of such lending platforms are Bitbond, Poloniex and BITFINEX.

Bitbond allows P2P (peer-to-peer) or person-to-person lending, both in bitcoins and in dollars, euros and other currencies.

BITFINEX is an Exchange service that offers the "Margin Funding" option, through which you can lend your bitcoins to people looking to trade cryptocurrencies with leverage, or "Margin Trading".

This method will be discussed in the next section.

On the other hand, the Poloniex exchange service offers the "Lending" option, which gives access to a section where lists of applicants and suppliers of cryptocurrencies or FIAT money are published.

OTHER WAYS TO EARN BITCOINS

Cryptocurrencies have become a real and practical alternative to FIAT money, i.e. paper money issued by central banks.

Therefore, they can be used in the same way as printed money for the purchase and sale of products, payment of salaries, donations and any other form of money exchange between one person and another.

In the wake of the Covid-19 pandemic, many countries saw their economies affected. To protect themselves, several companies started paying their workers and suppliers with bitcoins and other cryptocurrencies.

Although it seems risky, in reality what is sought is to avoid the loss of purchasing power of the salary (and of the company itself), especially in countries whose currency is devaluing rapidly due to economic problems, high fiscal deficits or even political instability.

If you are a freelancer or a specialized company, you

can start charging for your services in bitcoins or other cryptocurrencies, payable directly to your virtual wallet.

But there are also other ways to earn bitcoins with your individual or commercial work. Let's detail some of them.

Do you have a store? Get paid in bitcoins!

Many online sales portals have begun to charge their products in bitcoins or other cryptocurrencies, in addition to dollars or euros. Even food companies such as Subway or the computer manufacturer and distributor Dell allow their customers to pay in this way.

In the case of physical stores, it is increasingly common to find those that accept these alternative forms of payment. An important reason, in addition to the growing value of cryptocurrencies, is that payments made with them are not reversible, as is the case with credit cards or PayPal.

If you have a physical store, you can add bitcoin to your accepted payment methods, using your virtual wallet when charging for your products. For example, place a QR image of your bitcoin address next to the cash register.

Customers who have a cryptocurrency payment application installed on their cell phones or tablets will be able to easily pay by scanning this code.

Another option is to use an application that displays on a tablet or phone the price to be paid and the QR code that the customer must scan to pay you.

You can also use payment platforms such as Coinbase Commerce, which can be implemented in physical or virtual stores. This platform allows you to collect in bitcoins and transfer the equivalent in euros or dollars to your bank account.

Work online and earn bitcoins

In the last two years and especially in the wake of the Covid-19 pandemic, the number of people working as freelancers has increased.

In general, they use various portals to offer their services and attract clients and contracts. Although most of these sites negotiate in dollars and euros, many now accept the option of paying in bitcoins or cryptocurrencies for the services of their freelancers.

For example, the platforms XBTfreelancer and workingsforbitcoins.com stand out for offering the option of exchanging online services for bitcoins.

Use your blog and social networks to earn bitcoins

Social networks are no longer just for expressing your opinion or reflecting your mood to friends and acquaintances. They are increasingly being used as platforms for marketing goods, services and products.

The same situation occurs with blogs. From simple pages where everyone expressed an idea or talked about a hobby, they became spaces for the promotion and sale of all kinds of products, services and offers.

If you want to monetize the visits you receive on your blog, you can think about asking for donations in bitcoins or with a system that allows you to buy them using any donations you receive in other currencies.

Remember that the higher the quality of your publications, the more chances you have to receive donations in bitcoins. So make an effort and surprise your readers, they will surely thank you with their donations!

On the other hand, if you already have a website with a good amount of daily visitors, you can use it as a platform for bitcoin mining, using an external application for that purpose or a third party faucet.

For this you must add a code that activates the faucet within your website. Visitors will have the option to solve captchas, quizzes or any other test required by the faucet. The more visits and participations, the more tokens you will receive, which you can then exchange for bitcoins.

How to earn bitcoins through trading?

As with currency speculation in the formal exchange world, there are also ways to earn some extra bitcoins by playing with the price at which bitcoins are bought and resold in different markets.

The trick is to buy bitcoins or other cryptocurrencies when they go down in price and resell them when they go up.

However, the difference may be so small that it does not justify the effort. That is why it is best to have funds in two different exchanges and buy at a low price in one while selling at a higher price in the second.

PLAY AND BET, ANOTHER WAY TO EARN BITCOINS EASILY

With the rise of mobile devices and the emergence of increasingly powerful smartphones, interesting ways of earning additional bitcoins through online games or the use of apps have opened up.

There is a growing list of smartphone games that give the option of earning bitcoins without having to invest anything.

For example, we have the game Uranus Attacks (iOS only), which will give you rewards in bitcoins every time you recommend it to your contacts.

The Blockchain Game (Android only) will require you to "complete" a blockchain. The longer the chain you build, the more bitcoins you will receive as a prize.

If you like online games, we will tell you that there are several that offer prizes in cryptocurrencies and that may interest you.

For example, Satoshiquiz is an online game that requires you to answer questions on a wide range of topics.

Each correct answer carries a prize of 100 to 1,000 satoshis.

Gamefaucet is a portal where you will find five different games and a faucet that will give you cash prizes when you advance or complete tasks.

If you like gambling and online casinos, you will be happy to know that some portals of this type accept bets (and give prizes) in cryptocurrencies. One example is MbitCasino, where you can choose from 300 online games and place your bets in bitcoins.

HOW CAN I BUY BITCOINS?

We close this chapter by telling you about the process of buying bitcoins. First of all, remember to inform yourself well and understand the vocabulary and terms of the Alt-Coin ecosystem (chapter II).

It is preferable that you start with a small investment while you learn to master the terms and the way the Bitcoin market operates.

Buying bitcoins is as simple as buying any other type of currency online:

1. Enter one of the numerous sites that offer services for buying and selling bitcoins. On the Internet you will find lists of the most reliable companies.
2. Register as a user, confirm your email address and choose a payment method (PayPal, other cryptocurrencies, dollars, euros, etc).
3. Enter the amount of money you want to contribute as capital.
4. Select the option to buy bitcoins (BTC) and enter the amount of dollars or euros you will allocate to this purchase.

5. Ready! in a few seconds you will have a virtual
   wallet in which you will have your first bitcoins
   stored and from which you will be able to see
   your future operations.

WALLETS, OR HOW TO STORE MY BITCOINS

One of the terms that is important to understand regarding the use of cryptocurrencies is the "wallet" or virtual wallet.

For practical purposes, a wallet is the equivalent of the bank account into which you deposit your salary in local currency in a physical bank.

But in this case, the management and access to this wallet can be done through a program (software) or a physical device (hardware) linked to the blockchain network of each cryptocurrency.

Another way to describe a wallet is as software or hardware specifically designed to store and manage our private and public keys.

Without a wallet it is impossible to manage our balance or send and receive payments in cryptoassets. Hence the importance of using as much as possible the official wallets of each type of cryptocurrency.

HOW DOES A WALLET WORK?

Bitcoin and other cryptocurrencies are digital assets, i.e. they do not exist in the physical world and can only be measured, exchanged, valued and stored in the digital world.

Cryptocurrencies use cryptographic methods to ensure the quality and validity of each transaction. Remember that in the end, the wallets store the public and private cryptographic keys that each cryptocurrency platform assigned to you when you acquired your first assets.

These keys are the ones that certify that you have the ownership and the right to use any amount of cryptoassets that are transferred to your address.

This means that cryptocurrencies are not banknotes or coins, but a kind of "records" of transactions for and against you (income and expenses) contained within a blockchain managed and validated by interconnected computers around the world.

KEYS TO UNDERSTANDING HOW A WALLET WORKS

1. The private key is equivalent to a key, password or PIN and as such should not be disclosed to others. This key is what gives you the right to use the cryptocurrencies contained in a given address. Therefore, whoever has the private key will have full control over these funds.
2. The public key is the equivalent of a traditional bank account number. It is algorithmically derived from the private key, but you can give it to another person or company to send you a

cryptocurrency payment securely and without the risk of them tampering with your funds.
3. With the public key, addresses are generated to consult, receive and view the balance of your funds.

Wallets allow you to sign a transaction without the private keys leaving the computer where they are hosted.

By sending a payment to another person, you are actually transferring value in the form of a transaction, i.e., you are transferring ownership of an amount of assets.

At this point the network will need a digital signature to confirm your transaction and that the recipient receives the funds. And the wallet takes care of providing this digital signature.

HOW SECURE ARE CRYPTOCURRENCIES?

Thanks to the implementation and continuous improvement of cryptographic algorithms used by digital currency platforms, today we can say that wallets or purses are highly secure.

Every transaction within the blockchain is cryptographically protected at the highest level.

The digital cryptography process of a wallet begins the moment you set up your new wallet on a Bitcoin or other digital currency platform.

At that moment your private key is created using a secure algorithm, such as ECDSA or EdSA, among others, which allow you to create infinite combinations of numbers and letters.

This makes it impossible for third parties to guess your password, as well as complicating the job for anyone trying to do so using software or hardware for that task.

Once your private key has been created, the public key

is generated, which will be used to generate the addresses where you will be able to receive cryptoassets.

For this, your private key is used as a basis. In fact, both are mathematically related, but it is impossible to "guess" a private key from a public one because the algorithm used is unidirectional.

HD Wallets

There is a type of wallets called "deterministic" or HD wallets, which generate a seed when they are created. This seed is used to create keys and addresses and consists of a kind of word-based key.

If your wallet is stored on a physical (hardware) device and it suffers a failure, the seed can be used to restore or recover your wallet and the funds stored there.

WHAT ARE THE MOST COMMONLY USED WALLET TYPES?

Wallets play an extremely important role in the Bitcoin and other cryptocurrency ecosystems.

Due to the decentralized nature of cryptoassets, there is no controlling entity or body in charge of managing market operations. And this role is fulfilled perfectly by wallets!

Digital wallets have evolved since the creation of Bitcoin and the emergence of the first cryptocurrencies.

As the cryptoassets market became more complex and extensive, several projects began to appear to optimize and expand the functions of wallets. Let's review the types of wallets most commonly used today.

Full Wallets

A Full Wallet is the most complete type of wallet you can find. It is a wallet that works both as a node, so when you install it, it will download to your computer or device the entire blockchain of the cryptocurrency to which it belongs.

In the Bitcoin ecosystem, its Full Wallet is called Bitcoin Core and if you install it, it will download the entire blockchain of this cryptocurrency since its appearance in January 2009.

This represents approximately 400 GB of data! And this figure will grow day by day with new transactions made by users.

Of course, if you install it on your computer or device, you will be indirectly helping the decentralization of the ecosystem. But in this case you will not receive any token or bitcoin as a reward, since you would not be mining.

Instead, your role would be limited to confirming transactions and helping to decentralize the network.

Cold Wallets

Cold Wallets operate through hardware specially built to house them. They can operate offline, which also protects them from any hacking attempt.

Among the most used Cold Wallets we have the Trezor and Leger models, preferred by many of the investors who mobilize large amounts of cryptoassets.

Hot Wallets

In recent years, Hot Wallets have been developed, based on programs that can run on desktop computers, tablets or smartphones.

The development of this type of wallets has been favored by the remarkable improvement in speed, memory and computing power of mobile and desktop devices.

They are widely used by those who perform daily operations and remain connected at all times to the blockchain platform. Because of this they are more susceptible to attacks or hacking attempts.

Online Wallets

The fourth type of wallet that we can find today are the Online Wallets.

They operate through a website and often the protection of private keys falls on the administrators or owners of this site, similar to the way the online platforms of traditional banks operate.

Although they are considered the least secure of all wallets, most of them allow you to configure passwords and security layers to strengthen key protection.

5

SECRETS OF THE BLOCKCHAIN

The conception of the new cryptocurrency Bitcoin occurred in 2008 in the mind of an individual who went by the pseudonym Satoshi Nakamoto. Using a source code based on free software, Nakamoto worked together with several developers to create a cryptocurrency that was completely independent of any formal banking system.

But at the same time, this cryptocurrency had to be inviolable and have its own validation system and its own platform for storing data related to transactions and operations.

The operation of the Blockchain is based on a database shared among thousands of computers around the world, which validate each transaction made from the "virtual wallets" of users who make a purchase or sale of goods or services using this cryptocurrency.

This database has very complex algorithms and high-level security systems.

The security and independence of the Blockchain platform has led to implement its use in areas as diverse as finance, mining, capital investment, cybersecurity solutions, insurance, logistics and others where it is important to ensure the protection of data related to operations.

Thus, Bitcoin was born as a unit of account for accounting and transferring values, while the Blockchain is the platform that validates each transaction and certifies its authenticity and inviolability.

Like any other currency, the Bitcoin is also made up of smaller units of value. In this case, one Bitcoin is made up of 100 million satoshis.

And to understand why this cryptocurrency is so important, we will tell you that at the end of March 2021 each Bitcoin in circulation was worth US$52,872.27, making it the most expensive virtual currency in the world.

EXTREME SECURITY THANKS TO THE BLOCKCHAIN

It is important to delve into the Blockchain, because without this platform Bitcoin could not fulfill the premise of transparency and security that its creator promised at the time of launching this virtual currency.

As we said, a distributed database is used to keep track of all transactions or "exchanges" that take place within Bitcoin.

This database stores the information grouped in blocks scattered throughout the network and chained together, forming a data structure called "blockchain" or Blockchain in English.

This structure is best described as a "digital ledger" in which every transaction is permanently recorded.

In addition, the transaction history can be verified at any time to prevent tampering, theft or loss of data due to unintentional or intentional causes.

Blockchain technology was not created by the inventor of Bitcoin, although he was the one who gave it its first practical and worldwide use.

It is actually an invention of computer scientists and mathematicians Stuart Haber and William Scott Stornetta, who in 1991 proposed the creation of a blockchain of data secured with cryptographic algorithms.

The idea was to create a new way of managing databases in which no one could manipulate the timestamp of documents. This means that the content of a record can only be updated by adding another block of information and linking it to the previous one.

Furthermore, these databases and the management of the blocks of information would not depend on a single server or computer, but on a wide network without centralized control, in which thousands of computers share, compare and confirm the accuracy of each block of information.

In 1992 Haber and Stornetta modified the Blockchain code to make it more efficient through the use of "Merkle trees". This system allowed a larger amount of data to be collected in a single block, reducing the time required for validation.

Although it was the Bitcoin cryptocurrency that promoted its use on a global scale starting in 2008, the Blockchain system has gone on to become an independent tool used in finance, commerce and even education and health.

For reference, many experts believe that with the huge boost in digital commerce due to the pandemic, the use of Blockchain in financial, commercial, legal and real estate applications will grow by as much as 400% by 2022.

A CRYPTOCURRENCY IMPOSSIBLE TO COUNTERFEIT

Another advantage of Bitcoin and its Blockchain platform is that it has a proof system that prevents "counterfeiting" of cryptocurrencies held by a user.

It is also not possible to use the balance of the same virtual wallet in two or more transactions simultaneously.

This makes it invulnerable to many of the problems of electronic money handled in traditional banking systems.

In addition, being in a network based on peer-to-peer computers, there is no central computer or main node in charge of controlling everything.

The database is managed independently and autonomously, using point-to-point networks and a server that handles the time-stamping operation.

The blocks that form a chain contain batches of transactions that have been validated and approved by all the computers that join the network. In addition, each block is protected with a cryptographic hash that relates it to a previous block in the chain.

BLOCKCHAIN EVOLVES: ETHEREUM EMERGES

The ability of self-protection and continuous validation of the database used by the Blockchain has led to the implementation of this system in a wide variety of financial activities.

In the context of a world economy hit by the Covid-19 pandemic and the problems experienced in the United States and Europe as a result of the real estate bubble in 2008, it was necessary to improve the economic transaction systems.

In 2013 a new version of Blockchain emerged, called

Ethereum, which substantially improves its features and enables transactions on a scale thousands of times larger.

Its promoter was Vitalik Buterin, who contributed years earlier to the Bitcoin source code. Buterin felt that the original Bitcoin blockchain had not been harnessed to its full potential.

In this regard, he devised a variation that would allow the Blockchain to act more flexibly and be able to be applied in different types of transactions beyond financial ones.

In 2013 Ethereum was born, considered the 2.0 version of the original Blockchain. Among the main changes was a feature that allows users to register non-monetary assets, such as contracts and slogans.

The use of "smart contracts" has served to move this platform from being the basis of a cryptocurrency to the basis for the development of decentralized applications in areas as diverse as real estate, commerce, finance, healthcare and education.

6

WHALES, THE BIG FISHES OF THE ECOSYSTEM

If you read the alt-coin glossary in Chapter II carefully, you will find some curious terms such as "whales", "bears" and "bulls".

These terms already existed in the stock market world, in the trading of shares and commodities, and are now naturally also used in the cryptocurrency ecosystem.

A Whale is a term that analogizes to a person or group of people who own a large amount of cryptocurrencies.

They are associated with opportunism, as whales can use the capital they have in their hands to manipulate currency prices and make large profits, even in a single asset purchase and sale transaction.

Bulls, on the other hand, are the buyers pushing the upward trend in the value of cryptocurrencies and are associated with

In turn, bears are the sellers that cause their loss of value and are often associated with fear in the market.

Let's better detail what a whale is and how it operates. First of all, it is necessary to understand that they become visible when a major cryptocurrency is issued from a wallet or several of them belonging to an individual or institution.

Just as in the ocean the whale is the largest animal, here we are talking about someone who seeks to feed on the weakest thanks to his enormous capacity to buy or sell cryptocurrencies at will.

There is no concrete definition of how much capital a wallet must have in balance to be identified as a whale. However, sites such as Whale Alert, which is in charge of identifying and tracking these whales, has established a minimum of 1,000 BTC in the Bitcoin system or the equivalent of US$1,000,000,000,000 in other cryptocurrencies.

This already allows us to begin to better identify who may be a whale, since at the current price of this currency only large investment funds and hedge funds can move such large amounts of cryptocurrencies.

On the other hand, there are individuals and entities that act as whales but use the strategy of placing many orders to buy or sell bitcoins for little value so as not to arouse suspicion.

In fact, it is rare for an exchange to execute the purchase or sale of more than 1,000 bitcoins. And many whales prefer to conduct their transactions through third parties, if possible.

In any case, their impact on the market is remarkable. Whales can manipulate the cryptocurrency market by both raising the price and lowering it with large buy or sell orders.

WHY IS THE ACTION OF THE WHALES NOT PREVENTED?

It is difficult to prevent the existence of whales in the cryptocurrency market, since it has ideal conditions for speculative operations.

It should be remembered that this is a market with high price volatility, lack of central regulation, total independence from any type of bank and a relatively small market capitalization compared to FIAT currencies.

Various portals and financial analysis firms have tried to identify and list the whales that can manipulate the cryptocurrency market.

Although many whales act "under the table" and away from the public eye, it is taken for granted that the market is already manipulated in one way or another by 10 large whales.

These whales use all types of cryptocurrencies in their operations, but bitcoin is preferred due to its high value and level of use.

Analysts have determined that in the case of the Bitcoin ecosystem, the top 50 wallets with the most capital have enough hoarded bitcoins in their hands to manage this market at their convenience and without any resistance from other users.

LARGEST PUBLICLY KNOWN WHALES

Many of the largest whales are hedge funds and bitcoin investment funds. The best known and most involved in cryptoasset trading operations are:

- Capital Panther
- Reserve Bitcoins
- Financial binary

- Coin Capital Partners
- Falcon Global Capital
- Fortress
- Bitcoin Investment Trust
- Global Advisors Bitcoin Investment Fund

But it should be noted that these funds usually have some form of regulation that prevents them from managing the market at will.

Unlike those mentioned above, other whales operate anonymously using specialized methods to avoid detection before intervening in the market to cause prices to rise or fall.

Some portals such as bitinfocharts.com allow you to identify the 10 wallets with the largest bitcoin funds, but only those that are regulated in one way or another.

HOW DO WHALES OPERATE?

Whales make profits in different ways, but in general they apply a speculative method that is very common in the stock market world.

First, the whale starts selling a large batch of cryptoassets at a price lower than the market price, which causes fear and makes many also run to sell their cryptocurrencies, even at a price that leaves them with losses.

The whale keeps an eye on the market at all times and when the price has dropped sufficiently, it starts to buy back as many cryptoassets as possible, fattening its wallet considerably.

Subsequently, the whale will wait for the price of cryptoassets to recover and will be able to sell small lots at a good price, or it will repeat this move to increase its wealth even more.

Whales initially use coins with a low Market Cap, with which it is easier for them to make quick profits. Once they have increased their volume of cryptoassets, they move on to trade in the Bitcoin ecosystem, where they need to have a good capital backing.

The most commonly used low market cap coins in this manipulative scheme are Tron, ADA and Litecoin.

Another interesting point of manipulation comes into play here. To avoid their presence being detected or to avoid the risk that the exchange cannot handle a large buy-sell order, whales manipulate the market by launching a large number of small orders instead of a single large one.

While this may mean that it takes days or weeks to get asset prices to the level they want, they eliminate the risk of supply or demand spilling over in a way that makes it impossible to control the market.

HISTORICAL EXAMPLES OF MANIPULATION

In 2014, there was a massive sale of bitcoins at US$300 per unit, which led to a short stampede by bears (panicked sellers).

Suddenly, however, buy orders for 30,000 BTC appeared, which led to a sudden price increase to US$375. In total, the whales that made this move managed to earn US$11.25 million in just a few minutes.

In 2019 another case of bitcoin market manipulation by whales occurred. On April 6 of that year, 22 purchase trades in the amount of US$200 million were suddenly recorded, driving up the price of bitcoin.

In summary, if you are interested in investing your capital in bitcoins or starting to use this cryptoasset as a reliable future reserve, it is important that you learn to recognize the signs that market manipulation is coming.

In this way, you will avoid losses when selling or buying your valuable assets in conditions that are not real.

There are currently several portals and tools that allow those interested in participating in the Bitcoin ecosystem to recognize whales.

One example is the Whale Alert tool, which through its channel on Telegram or on the social network Twitter informs about the movements of large amounts of cryptoassets on the market.

7

WHO IS BEHIND BITCOIN?

At the beginning we told you that bitcoin was created by a person who initially identified himself with the pseudonym Satochi Nakamoto, an alleged 37-year-old Japanese citizen.

However, it was always speculated that perhaps this name did not represent an individual but a group of people.

But in 2016 someone appeared claiming to be Satoshi Nakamoto and many media outlets rushed to claim that the long wait to find out the true identity of the creator of the world's most widely used cryptocurrency had come to an end.

The one who claimed to be Nakamoto was none other than Australian billionaire Craigh Wright, a computer engineer who presented several compelling pieces of evidence to back up his claim of identity.

At the time, Wright himself claimed to own the equivalent of $761 million in bitcoins. And to prove his role in the creation of this cryptocurrency, he presented his evidence to the specialized magazines The Economist and GQ, as well as to the BBC in London.

What is interesting is that several members of the team who have worked from the beginning on building and expanding the Bitcoin platform supported it.

Added to this was the statement of one of the promoters of the Bitcoin Foundation, Jon Matonis, who claimed to have done an analysis that led him to the conclusion that the data presented by Wright was authentic.

"I had the opportunity to review the relevant data on the cryptographic, social and technical fronts. And I firmly believe that Craig Wright satisfies all three of those categories," he said.

THE HUNT FOR THE WHITE WHALE

But before we continue, we want to tell you that for years many specialized portals, foundations, experts and even the U.S. government have tried unsuccessfully to discover the true identity of Satoshi Nakamoto.

They have even said that it is equivalent to the hunt for the great white whale in the book "Moby Dick".

The U.S. newspaper New York Times hired Nathaniel Popper, author of the book "Digital Gold" about the creation of bitcoin to investigate who Nakamoto was and where he was.

Popper ended up making a fool of himself when he cornered a cryptographer named Nick Szabo during a technology event and said publicly that this was Satoshi and that his real occupation was a school teacher.

"I'm not Satoshi and I'm not a school teacher," Szabo calmly replied, leaving Popper looking bad.

The renowned Forbes magazine went so far as to track down a bitcoin coder in its early days named Hal Finney, whom it suspected to be the real Satoshi Nakamoto.

The Forbes investigative team eventually found Finney

at his home, but discovered that he had suffered a severe motor disability and could hardly have created the complex Bitcoin code.

What's more, Finney took a whole day to write an email response to Forbes using a transcriber based on his eye movement, just to deny that he was Nakamoto.

Newsweek magazine also made a fool of itself when in 2015 it claimed to have found someone named Satoshi Nakamoto and launched a headline with the "news". But in the end it could show no more evidence than the coincidence in the name, very common in Japan, and had to remove the article from its website.

ANOTHER POSSIBLE BITCOIN CREATOR APPEARS

At the same time that Craigh Wrigth appeared claiming to be Nakamoto, another alleged "creator of Bitcoin, a cryptographic engineer named Hal Finney, came to the fore.

Finney said that while Wright expressed some initial ideas that served as a basis for him, it was he who brought the Bitcoin protocol to reality with the help of other friends.

"I was the main creator, but I had help from many others," he said.

DOES CRAIGH WRIGHT HAVE MERIT TO BE RECOGNIZED AS THE CREATOR OF BITCOIN?

Before the Australian publicly claimed to be Satoshi Nakamoto, his name had already been unveiled by a hacker who claimed to have extracted data from Wright's computer that "proved" he was the creator of Bitcoin.

d

This hacker sent such data (emails, legal papers and

meeting minutes) to the portals Gizmodo and Wired in December 2015, which in turn revealed "the scoop" to the entire global community.

Shortly thereafter Wright himself was interviewed by the BBC, GQ and The Economist in a forum where he presented several seemingly valid pieces of evidence.

But he also had a very nasty reaction against a GQ expert who was not convinced of his identity, even though part of the Bitcoin technical team supported him in the interview.

In the end Wright left the event prematurely, leaving many doubts about his story among the public.

WHY IS IT SO DIFFICULT TO FIND THE CREATOR OF BITCOIN?

Although it may seem contradictory, many prefer that the name of the true creator of Bitcoin remains a mystery!

The reason is that they consider that the greatest attraction of this cryptocurrency is precisely its relative anonymity and the fact that no one can touch or manipulate it.

For example, when making a transaction the parties involved only exchange their Bitcoin address and the entire transaction is hidden from the eyes of third parties, including governments and individuals with hidden intentions.

This explains why Craig Wright has failed to convince everyone that he is really Satoshi Nakamoto and why the Bitcoin community insists on asking for more proof.

And this is where the catch is, as proving who created the Bitcoin requires a long and very complex sequence of evidence, documents and technical demonstrations.

In any case, Wright noted that he was not seeking to

gain some sort of power or moral control over the Bitcoin community in making his disclosure.

"I publicly disclosed my identity for the sole purpose of ending all speculation about who Satoshi Nakamoto is," he said.

8

SECRETS OF BITCOIN TRADING STRATEGIES

If you want to venture into the world of Bitcoin and cryptocurrencies in general, it is important that you first learn some tricks and considerations that you must have for your trading to be successful.

To begin with, we will tell you that there is no easy way to make a profit, since prices and profit margins vary continuously according to the supply and demand made by the users themselves.

To this you must add that every day a greater number of investors and traders participate, contributing to raise the price of Bitcoin and other digital currencies.

For this reason, it is good to know some of the recommendations made by those who have been investing in bitcoins for the longest time. Let's review them.

DON'T SPEND ALL YOUR CAPITAL ON A SINGLE PURCHASE

You may have seen how bitcoin is rising in price day by day and you want to rush to buy as much as you can, spending all your funds. Logic tells you that the more bitcoins you buy today, the more you will earn when you resell them in the future.

But experts advise to always leave a part of your capital saved and not to spend it all at once on the purchase of bitcoins or other cryptocurrencies.

The reason is that this will protect you from unnecessary risks, potential fraud and even the unethical behavior of some exchange managers.

Another reason not to spend all your capital is that by investing moderately you may earn less, but if your forecast fails and the price goes down, your losses will also be less.

A second reason to keep capital in reserve when buying bitcoins is that you can use it to acquire other cryptoassets that can have an interesting behavior and leave you with good profits.

Remember that you can always exchange them for bitcoins if you wish.

As for the amount of capital you should invest in the purchase of bitcoins, insiders recommend not to exceed 5% of your funds in a single transaction.

DON'T SPEND MORE THAN YOU HAVE

One mistake that many beginners make is believing that the cryptocurrency market can make them rich overnight.

This leads them to want to buy more assets than they can with their current capital and they start looking for other "investors" to lend them more money.

This is the worst thing you can do, as often the interest on such loans can far outweigh the profits from cryptocurrency trading.

In the end, you may end up in debt and have trouble meeting your commitments to investors and lenders.

The best advice is to spend within your real ability to

pay and reinvest part of your earnings to buy more bitcoins.

UNDERSTANDS THAT RISK IS ALWAYS PRESENT

Just as in stock trading or FIAT currency investments, you must be prepared for the possibility of an investment in bitcoins or cryptoassets going wrong.

When making a trade, there is no total certainty that an acceptable return will be achieved, even if it seems that your strategy is perfect. Remember that this is a market that has more risks for investors and traders than the stock or Forex market.

For example, there is the danger of falling victim to hackers, exchange scams or problems with the tokens you were expecting to receive.

In addition, the value of digital currencies can vary greatly according to supply and demand, even in short periods of time. This is why the advice not to invest everything at once in a single operation is valid.

If you want to be a successful trader, you must assume the idea that the main thing is not quick profits, but to maintain a stable growth of your account in the medium and long term.

DIVERSIFY YOUR INVESTMENT

Diversification when investing is key to survive in a market as volatile as the cryptocurrency market. This means that you should try to distribute your capital to buy different types of assets and not limit yourself to bitcoin, ether or any other in particular.

In any case, always aim for the most liquid assets. Bitcoin is currently the most liquid currency on the market, but there are other very interesting ones.

The more liquid a currency is, the less volatile its price will be. In addition, there will be less chance of fraud in its purchase and sale.

For example, if you buy bitcoins, you know that you will be able to sell them to someone else in the future. But if you buy an illiquid currency, there is a risk that you won't get a buyer when you need one.

COMBINES DIFFERENT WALLETS

A frequent recommendation made by experienced traders is to store your coins in a Cold Wallet (hardware-based) or alternatively in a Hot Wallet (application-based).

The Cold Wallet is the most secure, but offers less flexibility than the Hot Wallet. But if you want to protect yourself better, you can store your cryptocurrencies in both types of wallets.

For example, you can keep 90% of your bitcoins in a Cold Wallet, protected and disconnected from the internet for greater security. And the remaining 10% can be kept in a Hot Wallet ready to be invested at the first opportunity.

APPLY TECHNICAL ANALYSIS TO THE MARKET

A basic tip of any capital or stock market is that profits are most easily made by buying when the price is at a low and selling when it reaches the maximum.

However, it is not always easy to predict when the market is at a low or high. For this, it is useful to apply technical analysis.

In the cryptomarket the costs of the coins are published for all to see and there is no need to look for "offers" or bonuses as is the case with the purchase of any good or service.

There are several methods and analyses available that

you should review periodically to better understand where the market stands and whether the asset you are interested in is expected to rise or fall.

DON'T LET THE CURRENT TAKE YOU

Many beginners seek investment advice in the "trollboxes" or chat rooms available on many exchanges, where traders exchange experiences, opinions and "tips".

However, successful traders prefer to follow their own cryptocurrency trading strategy and never pay attention to what the crowd thinks or does.

Another beginner's mistake is to pay attention to the "mood indicators" that some portals publish and that supposedly reflect where buyers and sellers are inclined to act.

These indicators only show the intention of other players, but in no way reflect where the market will go. For this reason, you may be misled if you pay attention to them.

LEARN TO LISTEN TO RUMORS

As in the Forex and stock markets, rumors can be a signal that a price rise or fall is coming and should be taken into account.

If you feel confident and have capital that you can comfortably risk, you can practice "buying rumors", i.e., going by rumors and buying or selling before the market variation arrives.

Those who buy or sell on rumor do so without having data at hand to prove that a bullish wave is coming. But at the same time, they are the ones who stand the best chance of making money if this wave finally arrives.

The reason behind this is that rumors usually appear

just at the moment when trends are in their initial phase. At that time there is not enough confirmed data to support a change in the market, but if you know how to listen to rumors, you could get ahead of them to your advantage.

READ AND LEARN AS MUCH AS YOU CAN

Finally, there remains the most important advice from expert traders: Never stop learning.

Even the most successful and experienced traders are constantly learning to improve their strategies and have a better view of how the ecosystem works.

After all, the market is constantly changing and new forms of interaction and business are appearing all the time.

Learning also means keeping abreast of the latest news and understanding what changes may be coming - continuous learning will help you to always be on your guard!

9

HIDDEN PREDICTION INDICATORS AND ALGORITHMS

Predicting the price direction of bitcoins is a complicated task and therefore, a number of predictive tools and indicators need to be used to get an accurate idea of future market behavior.

There are a number of technical analysis indicators that help predict how Bitcoin and other cryptocurrencies will behave.

There are also so-called "sentiment indicators" that allow the market to be analyzed based on users' perspectives, fears and optimism.

Technical analysis indicators apply mathematical formulas to evaluate variables such as the price of a cryptoasset and display them graphically. And while none are totally infallible, they help to obtain valuable information and design a better strategy.

Moving Averages (MM)

Moving averages are a technical analysis indicator that calculates an average price that is constantly updated. They act in a lagging manner, as they use data obtained during the previous days and bring them to a graph that allows evaluating the cryptoasset's behavior to date.

In this way, it is easier to detect where the price is heading. In general, the data of the prices of the asset during the 20, 50 or 200 days prior to the analysis are used.

MACD Indicator

The MACD is one of the most popular indicators in the cryptomarket. It is designed to track trends and measure "momentum", i.e. whether the price change is slowing down or accelerating.

For this, it makes a comparison between the past price and the current price of the cryptoasset, resorting to exponential moving averages.

It is widely used to detect changes in trend direction through divergences, when the chart indicates one thing and the data indicates another.

CM Super Guppy Indicator

The CM Supper Guppy indicator allows to visually appreciate the price behavior of a cryptocurrency.

It is based on the combination of several exponential moving averages grouped into a single indicator. In fact, it uses 15 fast and seven slow exponential moving averages.

With the use of different colors, it is easier to see the separation between the moving averages and this in turn gives a very clear idea of where the price is moving or the level of volatility.

Fibonacci Indicator

This indicator is based on the Fibonacci sequence, a mathematical tool created by Leonardo of Pisa in the 13th century to predict potential support and resistance zones.

It is useful to determine at what level the price of a cryptocurrency may react during a trend change. It can also be used to find possible profit targets when a rebound or Pull-Back occurs.

Volume Indicators

Volume tells us how much of a cryptoasset is being bought or sold.

There are several volume indicators, but the most commonly used are the OBV (On Balance Volume) and the ADL (Accumulation/Distribution Line).

Finally, we have one of the sentiment indicators that help us predict how the public will behave, the Crypto Fear and Greed Index.

It is based on a creation of the CNN news network to predict stock market movements. In the case of the cryptomarket, it aims to measure the two emotions that most motivate investors to buy or sell: greed and fear.

Greed increases when the market rises and investors tend to buy more than they should in order not to be left out. On the contrary, they sell irrationally if they feel the market is going to fall.

THE BITCOIN ALGORITHM

One of the most frequently heard terms within the Bitcoin world is "algorithm".

This term is used intensively in mathematics, logic and computation. It is a set of defined, non-ambiguous, ordered and finite instructions or rules that allows solving a problem, performing a computation, processing data and carrying out other tasks or activities.

One of the characteristics of the operations carried out in a blockchain is that its content is digitally signed.

Bitcoin uses the Elliptical Curve Digital Signature Algorithm (ECDSA) and uses the SHA-256 cryptography standard to hash the blocks on the chain.

When a wallet is created, Bitcoin takes a randomly generated private key and runs it through these algorithms to generate a public key.

The Bitcoin protocol then uses the cryptographic value

or hash of this public key to create a Bitcoin public address.

Therefore, at its core, Bitcoin mining is nothing more than a mathematical operation, done with an algorithm that makes it virtually inviolable and unalterable.

The ideal way to break this security would be to generate the private key from a user's public key. Whoever holds the private key will have full access to the funds in the corresponding cryptocurrency wallet.

But the problem is that Bitcoin algorithms work in only one direction and while generating the public key from the private key only takes seconds, doing it the other way around would take centuries.

According to various estimates, the most powerful computer in the world would need 400 years to break in order to crack the security of a blockchain!

Could quantum computers break bitcoin?

Bitcoin mining is at heart a mathematical operation protected by algorithms. But some claim that a real threat to the sanctity of the blockchain, quantum computers, is looming.

A quantum computer could in theory reverse the process and determine the private key from a user's public key.

This would scuttle Bitcoin's claim of sanctity and reduce its value to zero in seconds.

In any case, it is considered that breaking a blockchain would require a quantum computer with a computing power of 4,000 qbits. The most powerful one known today has only about 50 qbits of power.

But it is known that there are already two algorithms for quantum computers that can threaten existing cryptographic programs, Grover and Shor.

Med Cibersecurity company president Rob Campbell

claimed that quantum computers can mine bitcoins much faster than any existing equipment.

But using the Grover and Shor algorithms, they can also serve to insert blocks from a pirate and override the trustworthiness of an entire chain in a short time.

However, this would not be so easy. They would need several years to crack a blockchain and by the time they manage to do so, the Bitcoin community would have improved its algorithms to prevent such attacks.

10

FUTURE PLANS AND FORECASTING

As we kick off 2021, the future of Bitcoin looks promising according to all Bitcoin insiders.

As we said before, both Bitcoin and cryptocurrencies in general came to change the financial world for the better. And this change has been expected for decades by a world that is increasingly interconnected and where physical borders tend to disappear.

However, the way in which the value of bitcoin increases or decreases will depend on the users themselves and the way in which they exchange this cryptocurrency.

Let us recall that the Bitcoin market currently manages a fixed amount of 128 million BTC for sale and exchange to users. According to several studies, this capital will be fully mined by 2028.

Thereafter, an impressive rise in the price of bitcoin is expected, unless there is some sort of consensus to increase the availability of this cryptocurrency.

But let's remember that in 2016 billionaire venture capitalist Craig Wright, who boasts of being the face behind the pseudonym Satoshi Nakamoto, predicted that by 2022 each bitcoin will have a purchase value of US$250,000.

For his part, U.S. billionaire Mark Cuban has stated that cryptocurrencies, and especially bitcoin, have a great future ahead of them.

Cuban has said that his business model includes investing in various types of cryptocurrency and even reminded that he still keeps intact the ones he bought in 2012 during the launch of the cryptoasset trading platform Coinbase.

"My cryptoasset portfolio today is made up of 60% bitcoins, 30% ether and 10% other types of coins," he said in an interview with "The Delphi Podcast."

He even predicted that by the end of 2021 bitcoin "will be worth as much as a Lamborghini" and by 2023 its price will rise to the level of a Bugatti sports car.

But what stands out most from his interview is that this entrepreneur whose fortune stands at $4.4 billion is known for his longstanding skepticism about the future of Bitcoin as a replacement to hard currencies, something he does believe Ethereum will succeed in doing.

However, it has considered bitcoin a better alternative to the gold standard for those seeking a good store of value.

THE FUTURE OF BLOCKCHAIN AND SMART CONTRACTS

Whatever the future of bitcoin, it is undeniable that the blockchain technology on which it is based has a great destiny and more uses for it will appear every day.

For example, there is an estimated 400% increase in the number of smart contracts to be made this year 2021 compared to 2020.

Smart contracts are agreements between two or more

people or companies, which are stored and executed in decentralized networks using blockchain technology.

Thanks to smart contracts, decentralized finance (DeFi) and non-fungible tokens (NFT) emerged, changing the way business is done today, according to Forbes magazine.

In conclusion, Bitcoin is here to stay and despite its ups and downs and apparent volatility, it has proven over the years that it is strong enough to lead the cryptomarket for at least another five years.

11

VOCABULARY OF THE ALT-COIN ECOSYSTEM

Before continuing, it is important that you know the technical terms related to bitcoin, the Blockchain platform and everything related to the use of this new type of cryptocurrency.

Many of these terms did not exist in the world of finance and IT before the emergence of cryptocurrencies. Now they are in mass use and virtually anyone who intends to use cryptoassets should be well acquainted with them.

A

Digital asset: Any resource existing in a digital form that can be owned by someone or that represents content associated with a right of use. A digital asset is a property and as such can be sold, bought or licensed for use. Some commonly used digital assets are cryptocurrencies, videos, images, sounds, web pages and electronic documents.

Airdrop: It is the method used by different projects for the free distribution of tokens to a series of wallets.

Algorithm: An algorithm is a set of previously written, well-defined, ordered and finite instructions or rules that allow carrying out an activity through successive steps that do not generate doubts to the person who must perform such activity.

Given an initial state and an input, following the successive steps, a final state is reached and a solution is obtained.

Altcoin: Fusion of the English words for "alternative" and "coin". It is used to refer to cryptocurrencies derived directly from the Bitcoin source code or other cryptocurrencies that may be variations or "forks" of it.

ASIC: Refers to integrated circuits that are developed for a specific function, or "application specific integrated circuit". In the case of Bitcoin, they are designed to process SHA-256 hash problems (for mining) in order to earn new bitcoins.

ATH: Refers to the all-time high of a price.

B

Bear Market or Bearish: Expectation of declining prices in a market.

Bitcoin / bitcoin: The word bitcoin is used to refer to the digital currency while Bitcoin refers to the network or protocol on which this cryptocurrency operates.

Bitcoin Cash: It is a new currency that emerged on August 1, 2017 due to the lack of agreement within the Bitcoin community on the scalability of this platform. Starting from block 478,558, the currency called Bitcoin Cash was created and started creating 8 megabyte data blocks instead of the 1MB blocks that Bitcoin originally used.

Blockchain: It is a distributed transactional database, formed by blockchains designed in such a way that it is impossible to modify them once a piece of data has been validated and published. It uses P2P (peer-to-peer) networks with consensus generated through a proof-of-work (PoW) algorithm. In addition, the blocks are cryptographically linked with a reliable and inviolable time stamp.

Private or permissioned blockchain: A blockchain in which the consultation, validation and participation of data are limited to a group of nodes or entities expressly predefined in a list.

Public or permissionless blockchain: It is a blockchain in which there are no rules restricting the reading of data, validation of transactions before including them in the chain. They are designed to operate in an environment with minimal or no trust and to enter and exit them easily and transparently.

Blockchain Tamper Evident: It is a blockchain in which any modification is visible to all users of the network, once made. Although this blockchain can be altered, this act will be visible and notorious to all participants.

Blockchain Tamper Proof: It is a blockchain with a very high level of security in which there is no possibility of altering any data or it is impossible to access the resources to do so.

Genesis block: Refers to the first block that makes up a blockchain. In the case of Bitcoin, the first public blockchain emerged on January 3, 2009, when the first 50 BTC were sold to the public.

Block Height: Block Height or Number of blocks mined after the genesis block.

Bull market or Bullish: Expectation of price increases in a market.

C

Public and private key: The public key is used to receive cryptocurrencies in a wallet (virtual wallet) while the private key is a kind of digital password required to sign transactions that allow spending these cryptocurrencies. Both are linked, since the public key is a mathematical derivation of the private key.

Open source: Refers to the software development model based on collaboration between individuals or groups, in an open manner. The software developed has no license restrictions and can be modified to adapt or improve it, provided that the improved result is made available to the rest of the developer community.

Coinbase: This is the main reward or financial incentive for bitcoin miners to put their computer equipment at the service of the network. On the Bitcoin platform, it is the only feasible method to create new bitcoins.

Cold Storage: Refers to the action of putting and keeping the private key of a cryptocurrency in hard copy or in a specific hardware or equipment for this task.

Confirmation: Each transaction carried out in a blockchain is confirmed once its processing in the network is completed and it is included in a block and this is linked to the next block in the chain. Confirmation guarantees that the transaction was not altered at any time.

Smart contract: A Smart Contract is a computer program that makes use of a blockchain to manage important data in a decentralized way. This program operates with real assets (real estate, money, properties, etc) using blockchain technology to make any alteration by third parties, fraud or theft impossible.

Like any computer program, it operates under premises and clauses that, when fully complied with, trigger the exchange of assets or securities between the parties, automatically and without human intervention.

They can interact with other contracts, make decisions, store data and send cryptocurrencies or tokens.

Cryptography: Data encryption technique using algorithms, which is used to make certain messages or documents unintelligible to persons not authorized to read or receive them. The SHA-256 cryptographic algorithm is widely used in the Bitcoin protocol.

Cryptocurrency: Digital medium of exchange that is used in public blockchains for the exchange of records. Unlike traditional currencies their exchange and value is not regulated by any central entity, such as banks or governments. There are many cryptocurrencies, but the best known are bitcoin, ether and digecoin.

D

DAO: It is a decentralized autonomous organization (decentralized autonomous organization) that exists on the Internet and operates autonomously but whose automation is not complete and therefore depends on people to perform some tasks. In general, they are organizations with automated internal capital but that need human beings in a marginal way.

DApp: Decentralized application.

Decentralization: Characteristic of systems that do not depend on a central or single point to function. It favors independence and complicates censorship and control.

Distributed Ledger: Distributed database maintained by each participant or node in a large network. There is no central administrator or centralized data storage. Requires a peer-to-peer (P2P) network, as well as consensus algorithms to ensure replication across nodes.

Address: String of numbers and letters generated from the public and private keys, which we could define as the fingerprint of these keys. The public address is a smaller version of the public key and is the one we will give to the network to inform them where to send the cryptocurrencies.

Chain difficulty: Represents the level of difficulty faced by miners of a blockchain when mining user transactions and adding them to the blockchain.

Double spending: This is a potential flaw of digital money whereby the same digital currency can be spent more than once in a decentralized system. The double-spending problem was solved with the emergence of Bitcoin.

E

Ether: Ethereum unit of account or token.

Ethereum: Open source platform, decentralized and based on the Blockchain model that allows the creation of smart contracts. It uses a PoW consensus system, although work is currently underway to implement the PoS system.

It uses a token called ether that enables the execution of smart contracts over its network using the Ethereum Virtual Machine (EVM). This machine operates in a distributed manner on computers assigned by miners, who receive ethers as compensation for their work.

F

Faucet: In Spanish "faucet", it is a reward system that operates through an application or a web page that gives away small amounts of cryptocurrencies to promote its use among internet users or to obtain some kind of utility.

FOMO: Refers to the fear of missing out on a price

increase or "fear of missing out".

Fork: This term is used to define a situation in which a blockchain is split into two separate chains temporarily or permanently. This fork occurs when the source code of a project is taken to create a new one that follows its own course.

A Hard Fork occurs when a blockchain splits into two separate incompatible chains, this is a consequence of the use of two incompatible sets of rules that attempt to govern the system.

A Soft Fork is a rule change that creates blocks recognized as valid by the previous software, i.e. it is backward compatible.

FUD: Fear, Doubt and Uncertainty. Refers to propaganda or rumors of market decline.

G

Gas: Internal price to execute a contract or transaction on the Ethereum platform. It is generally used to decouple the ether (ETH) and its market value, in order to measure the use of computational resources.

GPU: Graphics Processing Unit. Most tokens that require PoW as a consensus mechanism use hardware-based mining that make use of powerful GPUs such as those used in 3D imaging and gaming, which have the capacity to solve complex algorithms in a short time.

H

Halving: The act of halving the reward given to miners for completing a block of transactions. The design of the Bitcoin protocol establishes that the creation of new coins is halved every four years. This implies that the reward received by miners will also be progressively reduced.

Hard Cap: Limit of money that a project will receive from its investors through an ICO. When this limit is reached, the distribution of more tokens is stopped.

Hash: Fingerprint. A hash is a one-way function and hashing aims to create a fingerprint on the content to which the function is applied.

The resulting fingerprint will have a fixed length that will depend only on the algorithm used, whatever the size of the content on which it is applied.

Hashes are written in hexadecimal system using the numbers 0 to 9 and the letters A to F). The same set of data will always result in an identical hash, but if just one bit of information is altered, the resulting hash will be different.

HODL: Modification of the word HOLD. In this case it means to maintain your current position in the portfolio, without showing any intention to sell.

I

ICO: Initial Coin Offering (Initial Coin Offering). It is used to finance the development of new decentralized protocols in blockchain.

L

Lightning Network: Proposed solution to solve bitcoin's scalability problem, applying a secondary layer based on network protocol. Thanks to this, it allows to process payments and micropayments almost instantaneously.

M

Market Cap: Market capitalization. It also refers to the total supply of the number of cryptocurrencies or tokens, multiplied by the price of the cryptocurrency at the time of the transaction.

Merkle Tree: Structure of values in the form of a tree where each previous hash is the result of applying a hash function on the hash of hashes, until arriving at a root hash.

This allows many separate pieces of data to be linked to a single hash value, providing a way to efficiently verify the contents of a large database.

Mining: Operation performed to issue new cryptoassets and/or validate and confirm transactions on a data blockchain.

Miner: Nodes that participate in a blockchain performing the task of validating transactions and creating blocks, with the goal of receiving the reward offered by a cryptocurrency.

FIAT currency: Legal tender. It is issued by central banks, but is also issued by commercial banks when they lend to individuals or companies.

Wallet: Software that stores the private keys needed to access the cryptocurrencies registered in an address or public key to spend them.

Mooning: A situation in which prices rise uncontrollably, i.e., they "go through the roof" (or to the moon).

Multisignature: It is a form of technology used to add security to the transactions of a wallet, using multiple signatures. In order for such a wallet to be able to transact, it is necessary that several users approve the execution of such transactions.

N

Full node: A desktop wallet that maintains an entire copy of the real-time blockchain of any cryptocurrency.

Node: In a computer network, each machine is a node. On the Internet, each server can also be constituted as a node.

Nonce: A number used only once. It refers to a number that changes sequentially to vary the original message and cause the hash obtained to be different at each attempt. If the message is modified with a nonce, the resulting hash changes without altering the main part of the message.

O

Oracle: It is the information translator provided by an external platform and which is the only method by which smart contracts interact with data outside the blockchain environment.

P

Peer-to-peer: Refers to a peer-to-peer (P2P) connection or link within a network. In this type of connection all machines or some functions interact with each other without fixed servers or clients.

This term is also used to refer to a series of nodes that behave as equals among themselves and act both as servers and clients with respect to the other nodes, without requiring the intervention of an external machine.

Mining pool: A group of miners who agree to share rewards based on the mining hashing power they each contribute. They act cooperatively.

Transaction pool: Place where the transactions of a blockchain that have not yet been validated by miners are located. In this pool, miners choose which transactions to add in the next processed block.

Proof of Stake: Proof **of Stake** (PoS). It is a

distributed consensus protocol in which the probability that a staker finds a block of transactions and receives the corresponding incentive is directly proportional to the amount of coins he has accumulated.

The chain with the most support is the chain with the most "collateral" or stake. The staker needs to buy tokens to validate blocks.

Proof of Work (PoW). It is a distributed consensus protocol in which the string with the most support is the string with the most "work" or "hash rate" behind it.

It is a hash with certain requirements to make it difficult for the miner to find and the miner gets tokens from that blockchain as a reward when he completes his work.

Consensus protocol: Algorithm that establishes the rules that blocks must comply with in order to be admitted to a chain. These are the rules of the game that incorporate the necessary incentives to ensure that the parties are compensated for acting honestly.

R

Replay Protection: In the event of a hard fork, a Replay Protection or protocol is applied that prevents transactions of one chain on a different chain from being replicated.

S

Satoshi Nakamoto: Name (or pseudonym) of the alleged creator of the Bitcoin protocol and the software that supports it, Bitcoin Core. He first appeared in October 2008, when he published documents describing the operation of a digital currency system. On January 3,

2009, Nakamoto launched the Bitcoin reference software through the Souceforge portal.

Satoshi: Minimum fraction of bitcoin, equivalent to 0.00000001 BTC.

Scam. All those projects or people who interact with the Blockchain with fraudulent intentions.

Reliable time stamping: The process of securely keeping track of the creation and modification times of an electronic document. It is considered reliable in that it cannot be altered once it has been saved.

SHA 256: 64-digit hexadecimal hash function, with a fixed size of 256 bits (32 bytes).

Sidechain: This is an alternative blockchain that can operate with both Bitcoin and other alternative chains. In theory it helps to prevent illiquidity in the blockchain ecosystem and reduce volatility and market fragmentation, as well as prevent scams such as those registered in some alt-coin projects.

Soft Cap: Minimum amount of money established by a project to consider its objective fulfilled in the ICO. In general, the soft cap defines the minimum amount of money that would cover the execution of all the developments of such project.

Solidity: programming language used in the Ethereum blockchain for the development of smart contracts.

T

Game theory: Area of mathematics dedicated to the study, based on models, of decision-making and interactions in games. In this case, the term game refers to formalized incentive structures.

Testnet: Blockchain used for the testing of new code

by community developers without affecting the status of the community.

Token: It is a unit of value that describes a digital asset hosted on a blockchain that allows its owner to attribute it to a third party through the blockchain. It allows in its configuration several layers of value, which makes it a kind of digital trunk in which, depending on its programming, one or several rights can be included.

Tokenomics: Study of the creation of economic incentives based on the creation of units of value upon which self-governing business models can be created, empowering the user to interact with their products, facilitating distribution and sharing the benefits among all participants.

Transaction Replay: It is that transaction valid on the two blockchains created as a result of a fork. Sending coins from one chain can lead to sending coins on the new chain.

Turing completeness: Programming language that has a computational power equal to the Universal Turing Machine. System that in theory could perform any type of computation if unlimited physical resources were available.

Applied to blockchain technology and fundamentally to smart contracts, it refers to the ability of a language with this characteristic to be applied to solve any computational problem and implement complex structures such as loops.

W

Whale: Called whale in Spanish, it is an individual who owns high amounts of cryptocurrencies.

Whisper: Communication protocol for DApps deployed on the Ethereum blockchain.

THANK YOU!

Subscribe to our Newsletter and get a 30% discount on the next book from our publishing house.
www.nummumeditorial.com
info@nummumeditorial.com

We would like to ask you in return to rate us with 5 stars , to help spread the word about this work.
Thank you again.

◆ Do you often wonder what cryptocurrencies are?

◆ Do you want to learn to invest like a pro?

◆ Do you want to master these finances from beginner to expert?

◆ Do you know all the secrets to maximize your earnings and start making money?

✔ Discover this and many more secrets with The Crypto Code, a necessary compendium for our time, the techniques and secrets that have never been told to you. Do not miss this opportunity and multiply your income.